I0429211

Table of Contents

Introduction

The United States finds itself in the midst of a rapidly changing strategic environment. The erosion of traditional boundaries between foreign and domestic, civilian and combatant, state and non-state actors, and war and peace is but one indication of this change. Today, geographic borders have diminished in importance as non-state actors have increased their role in globally-diffuse terrorist networks and transnational activity. Across the US Government, all departments and agencies are struggling to adapt anachronistic programs and policies to acclimate to the evolving environment.[1]

> Dr. Robert M. Gates
> The United States Secretary of Defense

Today's strategic environment, as enumerated by the Secretary of Defense (SECDEF), is more complex than ever. This complex strategic environment affects the overall organization of the Department of Defense (DOD). In the opening epigraph, Secretary Gates explains his rationale for changing the functional structure of strategic communication and information operations within DOD. This realignment "assigns fiscal and program accountability; establishes a clear linkage among policies, capabilities, and programs; and provides for better integration with traditional strategy and planning functions."[2] Additionally, the Secretary assigns proponency of individual capability responsibilities within strategic communication and information operations to: Special Operations Command (USSOCOM) for Military Information Support Operations, Strategic Command (USSTRATCOM) for Computer Network Operations and Electronic Warfare, and the Joint Staff for Military Deception and Operational Security.[3] Secretary Gates is confident this directive will better prepare the DOD to operate effectively in the information environment to defend the nation and to prevent, prepare for, and prevail in conflicts.[4] The claim is that these changes will advance and integrate lessons learned into organizational structures and processes.

---

[1] Robert M. Gates, Dr., *Strategic Communications and Information Operations in the DoD*, 25 Jan 2011, Memorandum For Record, (The SECDEF, Washington D.C.), 1.

[2] Gates, 2.

[3] Gates, 2-3.

[4] Gates, 2-3.

Realistically, these marginal and incremental changes as directed by the SECDEF are possible in the short term, but changes in the direction of military force structure and how these forces are organized to perform their mission must be made through comprehensive changes to the Unified Command Plan (UCP). The UCP establishes missions, responsibilities, and force structure; assigns geographic operating areas of responsibility; specifies functional responsibilities; assigns primary tasks; defines authority; establishes command relationships; and gives guidance on the exercise of command.[5] The unified command structure is rigid, though designed to take into account United States (US) national security policy.[6] Title 10 of the US Code tasks the CJCS to conduct a review of the UCP every two years and submit recommendations through the SECDEF to the President.[7] These recommendations should take into account national security policy as outlined by the US Government.

Changing the UCP is not new to the DOD. Over three decades ago, a senior U.S. Army officer and historian noted that the problem of changing the UCP boils down to a choice between a total overhaul of unified command within the military, along with all its political liabilities and organizational dissension or, to a continual process of incremental change to the current organization.[8]

This monograph will examine what organizational changes within the UCP would enhance unified direction and increase efficiency throughout the DOD in response to a global or theater crisis. This monograph will propose structural changes towards a functional realignment within the UCP that will allow combatant commanders to achieve evolving mission requirements and objectives globally while still maintaining the principles of unified military operations.[9] With the changing global

---

[5] Joint Chiefs of Staff, Joint Publication 0-2, *Uniformed Action Armed Forces (UNAAF)*, (Washington D.C.: Government Printing Office, July 2001), I-2.

[6] Unified Command Plan (DRAFT 2010), (Washington D.C.: Government Printing Office, Mar 2010), 1-5.

[7] U.S. Code Title 10, Armed Forces, Section 164. Available at http://uscode.house.gov/ download / title_10.shtml, (accessed 15 Nov 2010).

[8] William O. Staudenmaier, "Contemporary Problems of the Unified Command System," *Parameters,* (Carlisle, PA: US Army War College, 1979), 93.

[9] Changes to the Unified Command Plan are drastic and costly. It is recognized that neither the Chairman of the Joint Chiefs of Staff nor the Secretary of the Department of Defense desires to fundamentally rewrite the entire Unified Command Plan because it will generate major parochial battles among the service components and strain an already constrained budget requirement.

environment in the *Age of Persistent Conflict*, the time to rethink and rewrite the UCP to establish commands based on this new strategic environment is now.

This monograph will be structured in three main parts. A review of current literature on this topic will round out the introduction. An important and detailed history of the unified command system will be addressed in the second section.[10] Tracing the origin and history of the UCP lays the foundation to better understand the background and differences in geographic and functional commands. It will also help the reader understand the importance of the command-and-control structures and the supporting and supported relationships covered in the UCP. The final section will address unified execution and command relationships of the current system. To complete the historical foundation, the author will address the current construct of certain functional commands in today's UCP in relation to efficiency and effectiveness. The examples chosen are Special Operations Command (USSOCOM)--an established functional command--and Africa Command (USAFRICOM)--an emerging regional command. The proposed new structure based on functional commands completes the argument.

Literary Review

The history of Service unification dates back to the relationship of, and the coordination between, the Department of War and the Department of the Navy. Books, journals, and articles written regarding unified command and unity of effort propose different models of unification for the military. The underlying theme of these works applies generally to a situation where a unified command is required to secure unity of effort.[11] These "situations" are generally thought of as broad and continuing missions

---

[10] A review of the major legislative changes to the UCP is outlined in the Appendix of this Monograph. Detailed discussions on the formulation, modification, and periodic revision of the UCP are cited in The History of the Unified Command Plan published by the Joint History Office of the Office of the Chairman of the Joint Chiefs of Staff. These documents rigorously detail the history of organizing U.S. Armed Forces in times of peace and war.

[11] Any effort to modify or change the existing command plan produces a storm of controversy, discussion, and debate. Some assert that the way a country makes wealth drives the way a country conducts war. For example, as commerce flourished on land, at sea, and in the air the appropriate military forces were developed to protect national interests and investments on land, sea, and in the air. Others argue that as the world is geographically split, so to should the responsibilities of the land, sea, and air components be split (and combined) across the globe. Other studies suggest establishing functional combatant commands (supported) charged to plan and execute with geographic commands (supporting) charged to coordinate and synchronize. Still, others suggest establishing

3

requiring execution by significant forces of two or more Services with a single strategic direction; by a large-scale, complex operation requiring positive control of tactical execution; by a large geographic area requiring effective coordination; or by using common logistics and supply.[12]

A few examples stand out from recent literature. Professor Dennis Drew from the School of Advanced Air and Space Studies addresses scenarios where the United States' involvement in crisis vis-à-vis national interests is ill defined. His book, *Making Strategy*, suggests that the strategies used to win maneuver warfare are quite different from those applied to counterinsurgency, and the military should be structured to both act and react globally. Professor Drew examines the military dimension of strategy (force employment, force development, force deployment, and force coordination) in combined and joint campaign warfare, and how the Services influence this strategy. He also includes basic approaches for designing operational strategy that proves useful as a starting point for unified command in campaign planning and unified execution in military strategy.[13]

Dr. Thomas Barnett, a senior military analyst with the Naval War College, writes of a "cutting-edge approach to globalization that combines security, economic, political and cultural factors" to describe twenty-first century war and peace in *The Pentagon's New Map*.[14] Dr. Barnett argues that the US should aggressively use its military to integrate dysfunctional states into the global order. Using Operation Iraqi Freedom as an example, he postulates this mission requires a significant reordering of the military. Dr. Barnett recommends a unified command structure by creating two distinct parts of the military: a quick-strike force and a system-administrator force to conduct nation building.[15]

---

dedicated responsibilities within the current construct of the UCP whereby the SECDEF pre-authorizes supported/supporting roles. And finally, as is the practice today, to implement incremental changes to the biennial UCP at the direction and discretion of the civilian and military leadership in order to keep pace with the changing and complex global environment.

[12] John T. Quinn, *Toward a New Strategic Framework: A Unified Command Plan for the New World Order*, (Defense Technical Information Center, Naval Postgraduate School, Monterey, California; Dec 1993), 63-64.

[13] Dennis Drew, *Making Strategy: An Introduction to National Security Processes and Problems*, (Honolulu, Hawaii: University Press of the Pacific, 2002), 10-15.

[14] Thomas P.M. Barnett, *The Pentagon's New Map, War and Peace in the Twenty-First Century*, (New York, NY: GP Putman's Sons, 2004), i-ii.

[15] Ibid.

These ideas build on the works of Thomas Friedman's *The World is Flat* as well as works by Samuel Huntington…both noted experts in US military history and strategy and both theorized the organization of the National Security Structure of the future. Huntington calls for establishing "mission commands, not area commands" because "the current structure of unified and specified commands often tends to unify things that should not be unified and to divide things that should be under single command."[16] Huntington argues that while some degree of divided command is inevitable, "the problem is to identify that form of division that is least injurious to the accomplishment of the mission at hand."[17] According to Huntington, geographic commands should be limited to regions where one mission is dominant.[18] This approach appears to tie vital US national interests to a system of limited geographic commands.

Articles and monographs also suggest drastic changes or minor modifications to the UCP. Captain W. Spencer Johnson, USN (Ret.), is a senior analyst at Science Applications International Corporation and also taught at the National War College. His article titled *New Challenges for the Unified Command Plan* defines military command structure and recommends apportioning responsibility globally. This recommendation realigns the Services to effectively address emerging threats with a capability to respond to surprises.[19] Additionally, Major Houlgate, a strategic analyst in the Plans and Policies Division at the US Marine Corps Headquarters and a member of the Naval Institute, postulated a new structure for the UCP in *A UCP for a New Era*. In this article, Houlgate proposes changing the entire plan to develop commands based on functional capability. He proposes a structure of eight commands divided by functional requirements. He argues that, with this structure, the DOD could mass experience,

---

[16] Samuel P. Huntington, "Organization and Strategy," Public Interest, Spring 1984. Reprinted in *Reorganizing America's Defenses: Leadership I War and Peace* (Robert J. Art, Vincent Davis, and Samuel P. Huntington, Editors), (Washington D.C.: Pergamon-Brassey's, 1985), 250-251.

[17] Huntington, 250.

[18] Huntington, 251.

[19] W. Spenser Johnson, "New Challenges for the Unified Command Plan," *Joint Forces Quarterly*, Summer 2002, available at http://www.dtic mil/doctrine/jel/jfq_pubs/1231.pdf, (accessed 15 Nov 2010).

effort, and expertise efficiently and effectively when needed.[20] In full disclosure, the author used this concept as a base for structuring functional commands as it relates to the current UCP's geographic and functional structure, with an eye on recent changes to the UCP and recent events to which the US military responded. The difference is this proposal takes into account recent changes to the National Security Council (NSC) and UCP while not diminishing the roles of each Service. Additionally, the number of proposed commands is reduced to seven to maximize efficiency.

Disclaimer

No classified sources were used for this study. The unclassified diagram of the operational command areas of responsibility and the 2010 unclassified draft version of the plan served to develop an understanding of the proposed structure in relation to previous plans.[21]

Strategic guidance inclusive to the UCP and outlined in the National Security Strategy, the National Defense Strategy, the Quadrennial Defense Review, the National Military Strategy, Guidance for Employment of the Force, Defense Planning and Programming Guidance, Joint Strategic Capabilities Plan, and Global Force Management Implementation Guidance provide direction for missions established in the UCP[22] but will not be addressed in this study.[23]

The study of the components of national security structures and policy shows the enormity of this field. In other words, the vastness of this subject is, in itself, a limitation. The background material displays a national security process that is complex, ambiguous, and constantly changing based on current

---

[20] Kelly Houlgate, "A Unified Command Plan for a New Era," *Proceedings*, (The Naval Institute:, Sep 2005), available at http://www.military.com NewContent/0,13190,NI_0905_Uni,00 html, (accessed 15 Nov 2010).

[21] The UCP is an Executive document signed by the President. The UCP delineates for Congress the coordination of joint military capabilities and operations across the services. Purpose, Concept, Initiatives, and Definitions are delineated in each biennial published UCP. Most changes are recommended by the CJCS and reviewed by SecDef. Changes normally are associated with internal concerns with regard to new or different threats, force structure, environment, or organization.

[22] Unified Command Plan (DRAFT 2010), A-1.

[23] Title 10 of the United States Code provides the basis for establishment of combatant commands and the UCP establishes the missions, responsibilities, and geographic areas of responsibility (AOR) for combatant commanders.

events across the globe. For example, the portion of this study that examines Africa does not take into account the recent revolutions in Tunisia, Libya, and Egypt.[24]

History of the Unified Command System

The following history of the UCP shows how unity of effort evolved in the armed forces. Early relationships were built within the Army and Navy when forces were combined in the War of 1812, the American Civil War, and the Spanish-American War. More advanced theories and recommendations developed during World War I, the inter-war years, and World War II (WWII) influenced the principles of unity of command and unity of effort. The National Security Act of 1947 (NSA) was the first legislative action to actually codify command relationships in the armed forces. The latest major change to the UCP, the Goldwater-Nichols Department of Defense Reorganization Act of 1986 (Goldwater-Nichols Act), clarified the command line within the DOD.

Over the past sixty years, studies and reports conducted organizational reviews and examined alternative reforms in the management and decision processes of the DOD. Most of these studies and reports reviewed resources, management, and command structures of the military. The most encompassing reviews occurred after major global changes that affected the construct of, in today's terms, the National Security Strategy. The two major examples include the NSA and the follow-on Key West Agreements, and the commonly called Goldwater-Nichols Act in 1986.[25] However, before a discussion of changing the unified command structure can be made, the conceptual background of the unified command institution should be understood.

The history of the current combatant command arrangement begins with the lessons learned in the Cuban campaign of the Spanish-American War. Between 1903 and 1942, the Joint Army and Navy Board sought cooperation between the Army and Navy, but accomplished little in the way of improving joint command. Decisions on joint matters in dispute between the Services went to the President. The

---

[24] The author suggests that historical changes to the UCP brought about by the military nominally fall short of the intended reasons behind changing the baseline structure of the UCP.

[25] Ronald H. Cole, et. al., *The History of the Unified Command Plan, 1946-1993*, (Washington D.C.: Joint History Office, Office of the Chairman of the Joint Chiefs of Staff, 1995), 11-12, 105.

President was the single commander in chief who had a view of the entire military theater and authority over both the Army and Navy on-site commanders.[26] However, one product of the Joint Board, an agreement on "mutual cooperation" in joint operations, was in effect at the time of the Japanese attack on Pearl Harbor in December 1941.[27] The Army and Navy commanders at Pearl Harbor were personally committed to the system of military coordination by cooperation. This alleged mutual cooperation failed. The Congressional Report on the Pearl Harbor Attack concluded that there was a "complete inadequacy of command by mutual cooperation" and that the conduct of operations was in a "state of joint oblivion."[28] Early in WWII, the Joint Chiefs of Staff (JCS) realized that the complexity of modern warfare required a unified command structure. The focus of the development of this structure was primarily military-to-military contact and engagement.

Following the experiences from 1914 to 1945, the Services recognized the importance of unity of effort achieved through unified command. Then, unlike today, the unified commanders reported to their executive agents on the JCS. Understanding exactly what role Service Chiefs had in the operational direction of military forces was frequently, and still is, confusing.

When reviewing the history of the US military with regard to the evolution of command authority among the service components, the DOD makes clear the importance of planning and executing joint, synchronous operations. The Joint Staff still cites examples of joint military planning and execution displayed by Captain MacDonough in the War of 1812 on Lake Champlain, by General Grant and Admiral Porter in the Vicksburg Campaign of 1863, and during the Cuban campaign in 1898 during the Spanish-American War as the origin of joint concepts.[29] These examples, both good and bad, gave rise to the Joint Army and Navy Board established in 1903. The purpose of this Joint Board was to plan joint

---

[26] Staff Report to the Committee on Armed Services, United States Senate, *Defense Organization: The Need for Change*, (Washington DC: Government Printing Office, 1991) 277-279.

[27] Chairman of the Joint Chiefs of Staff. History of the Joint Staff. http://www.jcs.mil/ (accessed 15 Jan 11)

[28] Ibid.

[29] Chairman of the Joint Chiefs of Staff. *History of the Joint Staff.* http://www.jcs.mil/ (accessed 15 Jan 11)

operations as well as resolve issues of common concern between the Services.[30] However, this Joint Board and its successor in 1919, had no authority to implement decisions or enforce policy. Without authority and responsibility, the Joint Board had little to no impact during the First and Second World Wars.[31] The Joint Board officially disbanded in 1947.[32]

Prior to the disbandment of the Joint Board, and with a requirement to coordinate administrative staff work while providing tactical coordination and strategic direction similar to the British military in WWII, the United States military adopted a *Unified High Command* in 1942.[33] Flexible and adaptable in order to react timely, this group of four leaders became known as the first JCS. Each leader was a military advisor to the president regarding military planning and operations.[34] The JCS grew in influence and, under the president's leadership, became the primary means for developing, coordinating and producing strategic direction to the Army and Navy.[35] The NSA codified this formal structure after the war. This legislation formally established the JCS as well as laid the foundation for the DOD as it exists today. The following principles from the National Security Act applied to the DOD: maximize autonomy permitted by law; no duplication in service, supply, and administration; efficient and economic command; quick and effective execution of top-down orders; and a simple staff structure with a minimum number habitually reporting to the Commander in Chief.[36] Additionally, the Act eliminated unnecessary and overlapping functions in the DOD while demanding top-echelon efficiency and vitality through the principle of decentralization.[37]

---

[30] Ibid.

[31] Ibid.

[32] Ibid.

[33] Ibid.

[34] Admiral William Leahy, Chief of Staff to the Commander in Chief of the Army and Navy; General George Marshall, Chief of Staff of the Army; Admiral Ernest King, Chief of Naval Operations; and General Henry Arnold, Chief of the Army Air Corps.

[35] Chairman of the Joint Chiefs of Staff. *History of the Joint Staff.* http://www.jcs.mil/ (accessed 15 Jan 11)

[36] The National Security Act of 1947, Available online at: http://www.state.gov/r/pa/ho/time/cwr/17603.htm, (accessed 15 Feb 2011).

[37] Ibid.

In 1946, President Truman approved the Outline Command Plan, the forerunner to the UCP.[38] This plan evolved through strategic planning for a global war with the former Soviet Union concentrated in Europe to become the foundation for the structure of the UCP. For example, the baseline structure from the UCP over the latter part of the 20th Century focused on maneuver warfare and Soviet-era doctrine developed by the Services.[39] Additionally, numerous force drawdowns and restructuring due to post-war lessons learned and internal bureaucratic and doctrinal infighting among each of the Services affected the plan. These factors, combined with budgetary constraints, shaped the UCP over the last sixty years.[40] To understand these pressures, this monograph will review the major changes to the UCP and why the Plan should evolve due to the changing environment for which it is structured.

The principle of Unity of Command is long recognized as key for military forces to operate in time of war, yet this principle is difficult to "translate into reality" in times of peace.[41] For example, during the inter-war years (between WWI and WWII) the Joint Board of the Army and Navy established coordination and mutual cooperation as the normal command relationships between Army and Naval forces. A more formalized, though temporary, subordination of one force to the other depended on which Service had the greater interest in the emergent situation.[42] This cooperation and understanding was "as needed" in time of emergency. Full subordination was at the direction of the President and usually an option of last resort.[43] Two emerging reasons changed this approach of mutual cooperation. First, the development of aviation and creation of an independent air service blurred the "line" where land campaigns transitioned to naval operations. The growing range and capabilities of combat aircraft changed how wars were expected to be fought. Airpower activists (in the Army and Navy) argued that

---

[38] Cole, 12-15.

[39] Cole, 107-108.

[40] Quinn, 63-64.

[41] Russell W. Glenn, *No More Principles of War?* Parameters, Spring 1998, 48-66. Available at http://www.au.af mil/au/awc/awcgate/army/no_more_principles.htm (accessed 1 April 2011)

[42] Kenneth C. Allard, *Command, Control, and the Common Defense*, (New Haven, CT: Yale University Press, 1990), 95.

[43] Allard, 95-96.

aviation would be the dominant arm of the future in both offense and defense.[44] Second, the rapidity of

modern warfare in WWII displayed that unity of command through a single, joint commander would

allow for the employment of resources and forces to accomplish assigned missions.[45] For the US military,

the transition from mutual cooperation to unity of command did not occur until after suffering numerous

defeats in December of 1941, most notably at Pearl Harbor. The divided command relationships between

the Army and Navy had parallel chains of command that only met once--with the President. The external

analyses at the onset of WWII shaped the command structure of the military. Because of this, the Chief of

Staff of the Army and the Chief of Naval Operations intended to institute joint command in principle

between the Army and Navy.[46]

Unified and specified combatant commands were defined in 1947 and the statutory definition of

the combatant commands has not changed. A Unified Combatant Command is a military command that

has a broad, continuing mission under a single commander and is composed of forces from two or more

Services. A Specified Combatant Command is a military command that has a continuing mission and is

normally composed of forces from one Service. There are currently no specified commands but the option

to create such a command still exists. The term Combatant Command implies a unified or specified

command.[47]

After WWII, and with the Cold War looming, senior military officials believed this new wartime

system of unified command should be continued. The major issue, as was the case with mutual

cooperation and coordination, was with the nature of the command relationship between fielded forces

and the joint force commander. The fundamental disagreement between the Army, Air Force, and Navy

was, broadly speaking, over how apportioned forces are subordinate to a unified commander. The Army

and Air Force argued to unify their own commands rather than by the geographic areas under a single

---

[44] Allard, 96.

[45] Allard, 96.

[46] James F. Schnabel, *The History of the Joint Chiefs of Staff: The Joint Chiefs of Staff and National Policy: Volume I: 1945-1947*, (Washington, D.C.: Historical Division, Joint Secretariat, Joint Chiefs of Staff, 1979), 173.

[47] Cole, 15-18.

command as during the war. The Navy argued that unity of command (within unified command) was essential for successful mission execution.[48] Generally speaking, these two preferences (regional command and functional command) shaped the UCP for the next sixty years. In today's terminology, multinational coalition solutions to recent events continue to restrict the US military from restructuring the current command plan because a region-by-region approach to unity of command appears simplest for the growing number of requirements with limited number of resources.[49]

The experience of WWII profoundly changed how each Service viewed the issue of unity of command. At the onset of the Cold War, the era of mutual cooperation established by the Joint Board was over. Further, the creation of a separate and distinct Air Force directly threatened the structure of the Army and the Navy. Beyond the strategic-bombing campaign, each service validated a tactical requirement for aviation. Post-war differences complicated inter-service relations, which resulted in the emergence of institutional independence from one another. The Army validated wartime experiences by preferring to efficiently manage and command their forces within a unified theater. The Navy believed that, with fleets scattered across the globe, task forces functioned best under centralized command of the Navy. As the emergent service, the Air Force believed in centralized control of all air power in both offense and defense.[50] Understanding these viewpoints (and how each set the stage for a series of debates throughout and after the Cold War) is critical to understanding the development of unified command and the UCP.[51] Also, understanding the strategic framework of the National Command Authority (today's NSC) as it relates to the National Security Strategy of the US is critical to understanding unity of effort and the UCP.[52]

The NSA established the NSC as the principle forum for considering national security policy issues requiring presidential decision. The NSC is responsible for developing, coordinating, and

---

[48] Schnabel, 173.

[49] The author makes this assumption based on coalition development over the last twenty years.

[50] Schnabel, 173.

[51] Ibid.

[52] Ibid.

implementing national security policy as approved by the President.[53] This Act established the Secretary of State as the principle foreign policy advisor to the President and the SECDEF as the principle defense policy advisor. Additionally, this Act established the JCS as the principle military advisors to the President, the SECDEF, and the NSC.[54] This basic framework holds the foundation of strategy development at the national level where foreign policy is separate from, though connected to, defense policy. To be clear, operational and tactical coordination remained at the Service and combatant levels.

The NSA was the first definitive legislative statement "to provide for the effective strategic direction of the armed forces and for their operation under unified control and for their integration into an efficient team of land, naval, and air forces." Additionally, the NSA codified the responsibility of the JCS to "establish unified commands in strategic areas when such unified commands are in the interest of national security," and the President would establish unified and specified combatant commands to perform military missions.[55] The military departments would assign forces to the combatant commands while the SECDEF would assign responsibility for their support and administration. Forces not assigned would remain under the authority of the separate Services.[56]

Constitutionally, the ultimate authority and responsibility for national defense rests with the President. Since the passage of the NSA, the President has used the SECDEF as his principle assistant in matters relating to the DOD.[57] The Secretary has statutory authority, direction, and control over the military departments and is responsible for the effective, efficient, and economical operation of DOD.[58] A recurring theme for this Act, and the other organizational adjustments that followed decades later, was

---

[53] Public Papers of the Presidents of the United States, *Statement on the National Security Council Structure*, (Washington D.C.: Government Printing Office, 1982), 19.

[54] Ibid.

[55] National Security Act of 1947, Available online at: http://www.state.gov/r/pa/ho/time/cwr/ 17603.htm, (accessed 15 Feb 2011).

[56] Cole, 11-19.

[57] Ibid.

[58] Ibid.

the underlying desire to create efficient and economical structure and operating policy. In doctrinal terms, this equates to unity of effort throughout the NSC and the DOD.

As the principle forum for considering security policy, the NSC has four statutory members: the President, the Vice President, the Secretary of State, and the SECDEF. The CJCS and the Director of Central Intelligence serve as statutory advisers to the NSC.[59] The NSA established the National Command Authority (NCA) as the President and SECDEF together with their duly deputized alternates or successors. The term NCA signifies constitutional authority to direct the Services in execution of their duties. Both inter-theater movement of troops and execution of military action must be directed by the NCA. By law, no one else in the chain of command has the authority to take such action.[60]

World War II and its aftermath provided the motivation for unification of the Military Departments under a single cabinet-level secretary. To establish this structure, the executive and legislative branches, along with the military, began an in-depth review before the end of the war. Service interests that reflected the opinions of experienced wartime military and civilian leaders (leaders with vastly different views of the postwar future) influenced these studies. Issues that dominated the search for a consensus included retention of air power in the Navy, maintenance of a separate Marine Corps, and the form and responsibilities of the new Department of the Air Force.[61]

The NSA incorporated overseas wartime experience beginning with the Spanish-American War. The result was a modern military organization. Unification of the Services under a single department became law and the responsibilities of the SECDEF were identified. The roles and missions of the Military Services (Army, Navy, and Air Force) were defined by Executive Order. The Act created the National Military Establishment (NME) under the leadership of a civilian secretary and created secretaries for the new Departments of the Army, Navy, and Air Force.[62] In 1949, the NSA was amended

---

[59] Ibid.

[60] Ibid.

[61] National Security Act of 1947, Available online at: http://www.state.gov/r/pa/ho/time/cwr/ 17603.htm, (accessed 15 Feb 2011).

[62] Ibid.

to change the name of the NME to the DOD and to recognize it as an executive department. Further, it changed the role of the Services within DOD.[63] Later, the DOD Reorganization Act of 1958 strengthened the SECDEF's direction, authority, and control over the department and clarified the operational chain of command from the President and SECDEF to the combatant commanders.[64]

The next major change to DOD and the JCS occurred in the 1986 Department of Defense Reorganization Act, commonly called the Goldwater-Nichols Act. The Goldwater-Nichols Act clarified the chain of command in the UCP while preserving civilian control over the military. The Goldwater-Nichols Act stated that the operational chain of command runs from the President to the SECDEF to the combatant commanders. The act also stated that the President may direct communications between the President or the SECDEF and the combatant commanders be transmitted through the CJCS. Additionally, the SECDEF enjoys wide latitude to assign oversight responsibilities to the CJCS in the control and coordination of the combatant commanders.[65] This Act expanded the previously discussed unity of effort with regard to command relationships to include the CJCS.

The command relationship established from the Goldwater-Nichols Act ensures that the combatant commanders exercise command authority of assigned forces and are directly responsible to the SECDEF for the performance of their assigned missions as well as the preparedness of their commands. Command authority may be delegated to appropriate subordinate commanders.[66] Additionally, each Service operates under the authority, direction, and control of the SECDEF. This includes all military forces within the respective Services not specifically assigned to the combatant commands.

---

[63] Cole, 19.

[64] Cole, 27-28.

[65] U.S. Congress, Goldwater-Nichols Department of Defense Reorganization Act of 1986, Pub L. 99-433, 994.

[66] U.S. Congress, Goldwater-Nichols Department of Defense Reorganization Act of 1986, Pub L. 99-433, 1014.

Combatant commands evaluate, plan and execute regional military exercises and operations.[67] This region-focused design intended to lay the groundwork to enhance the DOD's capability to coordinate and cooperate with various agencies to include the Department of State, US Agency for International Development (USAID), Non-Governmental Organizations (NGO), and Private Organizations (PVO).[68] However, these various organizations did not follow the geographic structure of the DOD. This resulted in a desired but difficult-to-achieve capability to coordinate with other agencies in government.

The Goldwater-Nichols Act ensures combatant commanders are accountable for performing their assigned missions. With this accountability comes the assignment of all authority, direction, and control that Congress considers necessary to execute command responsibilities.[69] This authority resides in law, Title 10 of the US Code, and in DOD Directives.[70] The Act defines the command authority to give direction to subordinate commands to include all aspects of military operations, joint training, and logistics; to prescribe the chain of command within the command; to organize forces to carry out assigned missions; to employ forces necessary to carry out assigned missions; to coordinate and approve administration, support, and discipline; and to exercise authority to subordinate commanders and command staff.[71] This combatant command authority (COCOM) resides with the unified and specified combatant commander and is not transferable.[72]

The COCOM[73] retains full authority to organize and employ forces that the combatant commander considers necessary to accomplish assigned missions.[74] The COCOM is not shared but

[67] Joint Publication 3-0, *Doctrine for Joint Operations*, (Washington, D.C.: Government Printing Office, 2008), II-11.

[68] Joint Publication 3-0, VI-5.

[69] U.S. Congress, Goldwater-Nichols Department of Defense Reorganization Act of 1986, Pub L. 99-433, 994.

[70] U.S. Code Title 10, Armed Forces, Section 164. Available at http://uscode.house.gov /download /title_10.shtml, (accessed 15 Nov 2010).

[71] Joint Publication 3-0, III-3.

[72] Ibid.

[73] The Unified Command Plan also delineates additional levels of control below COCOM. Operational control (OPCON) is another level of authority used frequently in the execution of joint military operations. OPCON is the authority delegated to a commander to perform those functions of command over subordinate forces involving

exercised through the commanders of subordinate organizations, normally the Service component

commanders, subordinate unified commanders, commanders of joint task forces (JTF), and other

subordinate commanders.[75] Direct authority for logistics supports the combatant commander's

responsibility to execute effective operational plans, maintain effective economy of force, and prevent

duplication of effort and resources. Services are responsible for logistics and administrative support of

forces assigned or attached to the combatant commands.[76]

In peacetime, the scope of authority exercised by the combatant commander is consistent with

legislation, DOD policy and regulations, budgetary constraints, and conditions prescribed by the SECDEF

or the CJCS. If disagreements arise with regard to the function or composition of forces, the assignment

of tasks, the designation of objectives, or the authoritative direction necessary to accomplish the mission,

the combatant commander may forward the matter through CJCS to the SECDEF for resolution.[77] During

crisis or war, the combatant commander's authority and responsibility expand to include the use of

facilities and supplies of all forces under their command. Joint doctrine developed by the CJCS

establishes wartime policy. In this case, the combatant commander has approval authority over Service

---

the composition of subordinate forces, the assignment of tasks, the designation of objectives, and the authoritative direction necessary to accomplish the mission. It includes directive authority for joint training. Commanders of subordinate commands and joint task forces will normally be given OPCON of assigned or attached forces by a superior commander. OPCON normally provides full authority to organize forces as the operational commander deems necessary to accomplish assigned missions and to retain or delegate OPCON or tactical control as necessary. OPCON is normally limited by function, time, or location. It does not normally include matters such as administration, discipline, internal organization, and unit training. Normally, this authority is used through component commanders and the commanders of established subordinate commands. A delegating commander can specify limitations on OPCON, as well as additional authority not normally included in OPCON. The term tactical control (TACON) is defined as the detailed and local direction and control of movements or maneuvers necessary to accomplish assigned tasks and missions. TACON is used to execute operations by placing command and control at the lowest level possible within the command structure. Refer to Joint Education and Doctrine Division of the Joint Staff. Dictionary of Military and Associated Terms. http://www.dtic mil/doctrine/dod/dictionary/ (accessed 15 Feb 2011).

[74] Joint Publication 3-0, II-6.

[75] U.S. Congress, Goldwater-Nichols Department of Defense Reorganization Act of 1986, Pub L. 99-433, 994.

[76] Unified Command Plan, (Draft 2010), 1-5.

[77] Ibid.

programs that affect operational capability or sustainability within the combatant commander's Area of Responsibility (AOR). As in times of peace, the SECDEF through the CJCS settles disputes.[78]

The underlying theme from the aforementioned restructuring of the US military created an organization where the effective use of the nation's Armed Forces required a unity of effort even though the organizations operate with diverse assets. The DOD expected to achieve strategic direction; unified command; and integrated land, naval, and air forces, all while coordinating combined operations and preventing duplication of effort.[79] Additionally, communications from the President or SECDEF to the combatant commanders may pass through CJCS. Activities delegated by the SECDEF to the CJCS can include the oversight of combatant commands.[80] The intent of the Goldwater-Nichols Act was to streamline the command structure from the President to the combatant commanders. Each of the Services continued to remain outside the command structure.[81]

Unified Command and the Unified Command Plan

Since unifying command was first suggested in 1946, the policy with regard to the organizational command structure for DOD has been debated. This topic of discussion will always be present. This continual plan, however, has seen the US successfully through every conflict of the Cold War and through the early decade of the *Age of Persistent Conflict*. This plan has been central to decision making and command and control, especially since the combatant commanders were greatly empowered by the Goldwater-Nichols Act.[82] The forecast for the 21st Century is filled with uncertainty and rife with expected and continued combat against state and non-state actors. Because of this, the senior military

---

[78] Ibid.

[79] The author refers to note 11 and the underlying question presented by USSOCOM 2011 Research Topics: At the operational level, command and control as well as support relationships need to be well-defined early in the operation. Examine the supported/supporting relationships between USSOCOM and conventional forces belonging to the regional combatant commander and/or Joint Task Force commander.

[80] Unified Command Plan, (Draft 2010), 1-5.

[81] Cole, 15.

[82] William J. Gregor, *Toward a Revolution in Civil-Military Affairs: Understanding the United States Military in the Post-Cold War World*, Working paper No. 6, (Harvard University: John M. Olin Institute for Strategic Studies, Aug 1996), 19.

leadership should re-evaluate the US' organization requirements and command structure. Clearly, the operating environment of this century requires establishing liaisons and maintaining relationships between military and government agencies.

This section will establish why functional commands are better suited in this day and age than geographic commands. Unified command and unity of effort in the current and proposed UCP will be addressed first. Then, two current combatant commands will be discussed: USSOCOM as a functional command with a global mission and USAFRICOM as a regional command constructed by function. Finally, a recommendation for functional commands will be presented for consideration.

The Services organize, train, and equip forces to provide to the combatant commanders of geographic and functional commands. Each commander is required to maintain a rapidly deployable JTF headquarters.[83] In the event of a crisis, the SECDEF assigns a supported command and gives instructions. The JTF for the supported command moves into theater to accomplish the required mission.[84] Using the Gulf War as an example, this effective military command-and-control structure can prove decisive in achieving both political and military objectives.[85]

The UCP outlines basic guidance to combatant commanders. Currently, six combatant commanders have geographic responsibilities. These combatant commanders are responsible for all operations within their designated Joint Operating Area (JOA): Africa Command, Central Command (USCENTCOM), European Command, Northern Command, Pacific Command, and Southern Command.[86] Four combatant commanders have functional responsibilities. These combatant commanders are responsible for operations relevant to their functional missions not bounded by geography: Joint Forces Command, Special Operations Command, Strategic Command, and

---

[83] Kelly Houlgate, *A Unified Command Plan for a New Era*, (The Naval Institute: Proceedings, Sept 2005), http://military.com. (accessed 15 Nov 2010).

[84] Ibid.

[85] Elliot A. Cohen, *Gulf War Air Power Survey,* (Washington, D.C.: Joint History Office, 1993), Vol II, Part II.

[86] Unified Command Plan, (Draft 2010), 1-5.

Transportation Command. The UCP directs that unified combatant commands be capped to a total of ten.[87]

Because the global environment is changing, the DOD should rethink the UCP to establish commands based on function first and geography second. An assigned JTF focusing on a much narrower set of operational tasks and missions would enable the JTF to better prepare for its assigned tasks and missions. Ideally, each commander would focus on a capability or functional area. This could permit the DOD to mass its effort towards expertise and economy of force. For example, in active operations today, most JTF missions require multi-functionality. Joint personnel, intelligence, operations, logistics, and command and control converge on JTFs in varying degrees depending on the mission.[88] Integrating these functions is difficult but not impossible.

For example, The Goldwater-Nichols Act required forces under the jurisdiction of the Services must be assigned to combatant commands, with the exception of forces assigned to perform the mission of the Services (recruitment, equipment, maintenance, etc.). In addition, forces[89] allocated within a combatant commander's AOR are now assigned to that combatant commander, except as otherwise directed by the SECDEF.[90] This is the structure of DOD that exists under the current UCP. As an example, the SECDEF[91] recently aligned the mission of strategic communication and operations under USSOCOM and USSTRATCOM by using a functional model.[92] This statutorily "assigns fiscal and program accountability; establishes a clear linkage among policies, capabilities, and programs; and

---

[87] Cole, 18.

[88] Joseph W. Pruher, *Rethinking the Joint Doctrine Hierarchy*, Joint Forces Quarterly. Winter 1996-97, 43.

[89] Bruce M. Lawlor, *Military Support of Civil Authorities-A New Focus for a New Millennium*, October 2000 (Updated September 2001), available at http://www homelandsecurity.org/journal/Articles/Lawlor.htm (accessed 26 Apr 2011).

[90] Cole, 13.

[91] The memorandum explained in the opening pages of this monograph refers to outdated programs and policies in response to the strategic emphasis to counter violent extremism from the National Security Strategy.

[92] Robert M. Gates, Dr., *Strategic Communications and Information Operations in the DoD*, 25 Jan 2011, Memorandum For Record, (The SECDEF, Washington D.C.), 1-3.

provides for better integration with traditional strategy and planning functions."[93] Additionally, the Secretary assigned mission responsibility to these combatant commands. Secretary Gates is confident this directive will prepare the DOD to operate effectively in the information environment to defend the nation and to prevent, prepare for, and prevail in conflicts.[94] The claim is that these changes will advance and integrate lessons learned into organization and processes.

A brief review of one of these components, Computer Network Operations and Electronic Warfare assigned to USSTRATCOM, might shed some light as to the Department's organization and process.[95] Computer Network Operations and Electronic Warfare are assigned to a sub-unified command subordinate to USSTRATCOM located in Omaha, Nebraska. This sub-unified command, US Cyber Command located in Fort Meade, Maryland, plans, coordinates, integrates, synchronizes, and conducts activities to operate and defend DOD networks and, when directed, is prepared to conduct military cyber operations in order to ensure US and Allied freedom of action in cyberspace while denying the same to adversaries.[96] The Joint Electronic Warfare Division, located in San Antonio, Texas, is assigned to USSTRATCOM to work in concert with US Cyber Command. The other divisions of this Joint Operations Center will be aligned with the Joint Staff located in The Pentagon, Washington, D.C.[97] With this example alone, and without addressing the added structure of each of the Service's major commands supporting the sub-unified commands, the challenges of communicating among the dislocated regional command system is apparent. Originally, unified commands were established to wage war in a distinct geographical area, focused on a clear threat, and with a finite objective. In the global world today, the lines of geography tend to be more and more blurred.

---

[93] Gates, 2.

[94] Gates, 2-3.

[95] This review shows one example of how the major commands of the Services are geographically split from the unified and specified commands of the joint staff and how the interaction between each, under a combatant command, is obstructed by distance and communication.

[96] U.S. Department of Defense, Cyber Command Fact Sheet, May 21, 2010, http://www.stratcom. mil /factsheets/ cyber_Command,. (accessed 12 Feb 2011).

[97] Gates, 2.

In an effort to become more "Joint," the Goldwater-Nichols Act of 1986 delegated priorities by establishing levels of operational and tactical control outside the scope of the military chain of command. This directly affects unity of effort.[98] As such, from the NSA, to the Goldwater-Nichols Act, and through the subsequent unclassified draft of the latest revised UCP of 2010, unified combatant commands appear to be neither structured nor designed for efficient unified military operations.

A unified military operation in this study is the concept of planning, synchronizing, integrating, and executing joint military operations. Unless specifically authorized by the SECDEF, functional commanders do not have the authority to execute missions globally. That authority remains with the geographic commanders.[99] The supporting and supported relationship outlined in the UCP creates friction along the seams of the functional and geographic combatant commanders and appears to impede unified military operations.[100] Special operations in Iraq and Afghanistan are a recent example of this issue.

Special Operations Command is tasked to conduct operations in support of the war on terrorism.[101] When these operations fall within Central Command's AOR, an additional level of coordination and approval is required prior to conducting these operations. This additional level adds precious time to the already constrained time-sensitive targeting process. As such, Special Operations Forces (SOF) leadership questions the ill-defined supported and supporting relationships between SOF and conventional forces that belong to regional combatant commanders.[102] To SOF, this requirement goes against Joint Doctrine and hinders unity of command. According to Joint Doctrine, unified action through unified direction is to assign a mission to a single commander and provide that commander with sufficient forces and authorities required for successful mission accomplishment. Furthermore, unified

---

[98] Cole, 11-19.

[99] Unified Command Plan, (Draft 2010), 1-5.

[100] U.S. Africa Command J5, Discussion with SAMS Fellows. Lecture, Kelly Barracks, Germany. Nov 2010.

[101] *USSOCOM Posture Statement*. USSOCOM. 2007. Archived from the original on February 27, 2008. http://www.socom.mil/Docs/USSOCOM_Posture_Statement_2007.pdf. (Accessed 26 Apr 2011).

[102] Kenneth H. Poole, *USSOCOM Research Topics 2011*, Joint Special Operations University, (Hurlburt Field, FL: Government Printing Office, June 2010), 72.

direction requires a mission, force structure (organization), and authorities (command and control).[103] Currently, a functional command operating within a regional command's AOR is inefficient.

In these examples, the current command-and-control system relies on the proper balance of resources, the right type and number of personnel, and the proper organizational structure in which to place the people, equipment, parts, and supply. The desire is to create certainty in command and control where collecting and synthesizing information and reacting with confidence in a timely manner is usually successful. Certainty in command and control is achieved by balancing functional and geographic responsibilities considering specialized and general-purpose capabilities. This "certainty" is invested in an effective military command-and-control structure that can prove decisive in achieving both political and military objectives.

There have been successful functionally based command approaches beyond Secretary Gates' recent memorandum. For example, during the 1996 Atlanta Olympics, the military formed and led a Response Task Force designed specifically to work with federal, state, and local civilian officials. Staff officers and personnel were temporarily reassigned from other duties to work for this task force. The Response Task Force's standup in advance of the actual event enabled its personnel to train in civilian response methods and DOD military support procedures. The value added by such an approach was quickly recognized. A second Response Task Force to cover response requirements west of the Mississippi was also created. The Response Task Forces represent a substantial improvement over the previous method of using ad hoc JTFs to oversee military support.[104] As part of a functional command, a standing JTF would focus on operations and issues to lend support to civil authorities. The result of this concentration of focus is an improved capability to bring military support quickly and efficiently in time of need.

---

[103] United States Army Field Manual 3-0 (FM 3-0), *Operations*, (Washington D.C.: Government Printing Office, February 2010), B-1.

[104] Bruce M. Lawlor, *Military Support of Civil Authorities-A New Focus for a New Millennium*, October 2000 (Updated September 2001), available at http://www homelandsecurity.org/journal/Articles/Lawlor.htm (accessed 26 Apr 2011).

In this proposal, a command established to assist with civil disaster relief would collaborate with, and have close ties to, NGOs. A command established to assist with security and stability could potentially participate in the US security cooperation and engagement efforts worldwide and have close ties to the State Department and USAID. As argued later in this monograph, both of these commands could have regional and global responsibilities. The goal would be to align and revitalize other elements of national power across the NSC. The SECDEF, in conjunction with the Secretary of State, and along with the JCS, could then allocate missions to commands and minimize risk.

Similar designs were outlined in the past. For example, during WWII, the Navy and the Army Air Force established an agreement in principle that land-based bombers, though primarily designed for strategic bombing, could accomplish anti-submarine missions under the operational control of the Navy. The Army Air Force recognized[105] the unique needs of a commander at sea requiring control of land-based combat aviation to perform naval missions. On the same token, the Navy agreed that the land-based bombers under their control would not conduct strategic-bombing missions.[106] This compromise is foundational for understanding Joint Command by function versus geography. However, it should also be noted that, even though the Air Force and Navy compromised in this arrangement, all three Services still fought bitterly over how to define unity of command and how to establish a pattern of unified command during (and after) WWII.

As in the previous example, the process goal was interagency cooperation. To streamline the most senior interagency organization that is responsible "to the President with respect to national security, so as to enable the military Services and the other departments and agencies of the government to cooperate

---

[105] Current Air Force Doctrine Documents regarding Counter Sea Operations detail similar arrangements between the Services but do not define command relationships within mission specific terms.

[106] Maurice Matloff and Edwin M. Snell, *The United States Army in World War II: The War Department: Strategic Planning for Coalition Warfare, 1941-1942*, (Washington, DC: Office of the Chief of Military History, Department of the Army, 1953), 49.

more effectively in matters involving national security."[107] In reality, this process is hierarchical. The following examples of USSOCOM and USAFRICOM show this hierarchical process.

A Functional Command Structured Globally: USSOCOM

The current UCP is based on geographically oriented (Northern, Southern, Central, European, and Pacific) and functionally based (Joint Forces, Special Operations, Strategic, and Transportation) commands. It is important to note that the geographic commands are based on 20th Century nation-state boundaries.[108] Simple map drawing is easy when a single "crisis" occurs. However, when the enemy is global and not belonging to any one nation-state, the map becomes less simple. For example, Hamas has ties to Lebanon, Palestine and the apparent backing of Iran. Al Qaeda operates without borders within failed or failing states. Humanitarian relief and disaster response knows no boundaries. To dig a little deeper, the remainder of this analysis will present a capabilities-based approach to functionally oriented combatant commands and compare it to the recently established, and fully operationally capable, USAFRICOM. The functional commands will be both real (Special Forces Command) and fictional (security and stability).

Since 2001, the US' response to leading the fight against terrorism has been USSOCOM.[109] The USSOCOM'S success compels the argument involving function over geography. The USSOCOM's apparent friction vis-à-vis the geographic commands compels the argument as well. The USSOCOM is a functional command that has a strategic war-fighting mission. This is one of the few missions outlined directly in the National Security Strategy. This command is well established and growing in capabilities to meet the demand of the current wars.

---

[107] National Security Council, *Handbook for Interagency Management of Complex Contingency Operations*, (Washington, DC: Government Printing Office, August 2008). Internet accessed Feb 15, 2011.

[108] Kelly Houlgate, *A Unified Command Plan for a New Era*, The Naval Institute: Proceedings, Sep 2005, available at http://www military.com NewContent/0,13190,NI_0905_Uni,00 html, (accessed 15 Nov 2010).

[109] *USSOCOM Posture Statement*. USSOCOM. 2007. Archived from the original on February 27, 2008. http://www.socom.mil/Docs/USSOCOM_Posture_Statement_2007.pdf. (Accessed 26 Apr 2011).

Joint and interagency partners predict a future of persistent conflict with irregular or hybrid threats in an irregular warfare environment, which will require forces to operate across the spectrum of military operations.[110] The USSOCOM understands this vision by educating, organizing, training, equipping, and deploying special operations forces in support missions to counter these threats. These forces are uniquely qualified to operate in small elements within complex, uncertain environments.[111] Core missions for special operations are foreign internal defense, unconventional warfare, counterterrorism, and counterinsurgency.[112] These operators are characterized by mature, astute, and lethal forces that capitalize on access and mobility to quickly and decisively accomplish the assigned mission.[113] This is a high-end capability to defeat threats to national interests. However, as enumerated by the commander of USSOCOM, most special operations require conventional assistance.[114]

The USSOCOM is tasked to organize, train, and equip its special operators. This gives the operators a foot in the door during the programmatic process to ensure moneys are available to accomplish this task. However, when these operators are tasked to accomplish missions in a regional commander's AOR, and especially when assistance is required, the parochial battles of supporting and supported relationships surface quickly. Typically, the organization of a JTF establishes these relationships between commands. As an example, if two functional commands are required to accomplish an assigned task, the SECDEF would delineate this relationship at the time of tasking. This requirement would hold true in the proposed plan in this monograph. However, USSOCOM can possibly infringe, in the mind of the regional command, on the proper owner of the AOR. This relationship is delicate and, if not thought about well before, can be disastrous for unity of effort and efficiency. This similar relationship is apparent within USAFRICOM from an interagency point of view.

---

[110] John F. Mulholland, Jr., "Countering Irregular Threats: The Army Special Operations Contribution," *Joint Forces Quarterly*, 1st quarter 2010, 71.

[111] Ibid.

[112] Mulholland, 72.

[113] Mulholland, 74.

[114] Commander, U.S. Special Operations Command, *Fifth SOF Truth*, "O" Flake, Number 09-13, June 19, 2009.

A Regional Command Structured by Function: USAFRICOM

President George Bush announced the establishment of USAFRICOM in early 2007. From initially operating as a sub-unified command under European Command to a fully operation regional command in under a year, USAFRICOM is significant to the US and Africa. The continuing and growing strategic importance of Africa and the creation of this command reflect a change in attitude within DOD.[115] The USAFRICOM is somewhat of a hybrid command. Though established as a regional command, it is structured to align core functions with engagement policy in the region. With this change, DOD appears to recognize that it should be proactive with regard to African issues by structuring USAFRICOM to assist the US Government across all of the instruments of national power.

The USAFRICOM also symbolizes change within the DOD with regard to structuring regional combatant commands. The responsibilities USAFRICOM possesses are that of traditional combatant commands but, USAFRICOM has additional staff billets to provide for more civil-military relations and capabilities in Africa. For example, the commander of USAFRICOM has two deputies, one for military operations and one for civil-military activities. This is a significant difference that some view as transformational regarding the DOD and interagency cooperative relationships.[116]

As a regional command, USAFRICOM hopes to reinforce conflict prevention by shaping the environment. According to this strategy, USAFRICOM will work with counterparts in the State Department and in USAID to ensure resources and capabilities, which promote diplomacy and development programs (and democracy), are used on the continent.[117] Previously divided between three geographic combatant commands, USAFRICOM focuses resources, capabilities, and efforts of one combatant command in Africa.[118]

---

[115] Stephen J. Morrison and Kathleen Hicks, *Integrating 21st Century Development and Security Assistance, Final Report*, (Washington D.C.: Center for Strategic and International Studies, Dec 2007).

[116] Mark Bellamy, *Africa Command: An Idea Whose Time has come?* (Internet accessed Feb 15, 2011).

[117] Lauren Ploch, *Africa Command US Strategic Interests and the Role of the US Military in Africa*; Library of Congress, July 6, 2007 (updated Dec 7, 2007; Internet accessed Nov 2010).

[118] Ibid.

To USAFRICOM,[119] tensions between command responsibilities, service requirements, and interagency coordination potentially hinder political development.[120] USAFRICOM's primary mission is to cooperate in coordination with diplomatic and international organizations.[121] The US Government's intent is to assist Africans in providing their own security and stability and to prevent conditions that could either lead to conflict or promulgate terrorism.[122]

The US-African policy attempts to address African security from an African-centric perspective. However, USAFRICOM is currently limited to a headquarters staff that does not have the legal authority, (let alone the structure, training, or resources) to support African governments in a time of crisis or need.[123] In this light, the US cannot "do more with less" with "efficiency" and "synergy" when it comes to security and protection in the region. Finances are limited, and the concepts of a comprehensive approach and active security are lacking at the operational level. The US "opted out" of Africa decades ago but, by creating a regional COCOM, appears to reverse that policy today. As such, USAFRICOM appears on task to use all the elements of national power. Unfortunately, USAFRICOM is not equipped to accomplish this mission fully.

---

[119] This analysis stems from research with regard to the African continent and the nation-states in whole prior to the developing situation in the north in the spring of 2011. The recent established no-fly zone in Libya, with the United States now in a supporting role, was not considered at the time of this writing.

[120] As part of the Advanced Operational Art & Science Fellowship curriculum, the class 2010-11 students traveled to numerous combatant (unified and sub-unified), and major commands. J-Staff leadership briefed roles and responsibilities at each location. The underlying theme as ascertained by this USAF Officer is that operations across the seams of geographic commands, operations across the Services, and operations across the interagency (cooperation and coordination) is lagging in capability. Additionally, duplication of effort within and among the commands is prevalent. For example, both intelligence and strategy sections have identical staff components at each the Joint and Service levels as well as interagency. The "walk-away" perception was one of duplication of effort (definitely not unity of effort).

[121] U.S. Department of Defense, *Africa Command Fact Sheet*, June 26, 2010, http://www.africom.mil/, accessed Oct 15, 2010.

[122] *National Security Strategy*, (Washington D.C.: The White House, May 2010), 11.

[123] U.S. Africa Command J5, Discussion with SAMS Fellows. Lecture, Kelly Barracks, Germany, Nov 2010.

The last two presidential administrations shifted African regional policy toward proactive peacetime engagement by expanding the military's mission to diplomatic and political roles.[124] According to regional experts, this mission attempts to establish provincial security from competent and legitimate governance. The result was a significant improvement in governance and in the number of conflict-prevention initiatives that included humanitarian missions, peacekeeping operations, and peace-building operations.[125] Accordingly, military-to-military programs in Africa proved counterproductive without broader political and economic development.[126] The one drawback to this functional structure is, to Africans, it appears that the US militarized foreign policy in Africa.[127] Unfortunately, this created tension vis-à-vis unified command responsibilities and interagency coordination early in the process that subsequently stymied political development.[128]

Contrary to local stigma (within Africa), USAFRICOM's primary goal is not to first use military force in response to crisis, but to cooperate on four major focus areas in coordination with diplomatic and international organizations. This requires the military to use an indirect approach. The four major focus areas of this command as briefed during a site visit are: building partner capacity; professionalizing militaries; improving defense institutions; and information operations.[129] The USAFRICOM is to accomplish this in coordination and cooperation with interagency and African partners. Unfortunately, while the "ends" are noble, the "ways" and "means" are lacking. First, USAFRICOM has no assigned forces. If required, USAFRICOM must submit a request for forces to other component commands and the

---

[124] Dennis R. Penn, *Africa Command and the Militarization of U.S. Foreign Policy*, (Washington D.C.: Department of Defense, July 2003), 47.

[125] Alan Bryden, *Challenges of Security Sector Governance in West Africa*, Geneva Center for the Democratic Control of Armed Forces, PDF available at http://www.ssrnetwork.net/document_library (accessed 15 Oct 2010).

[126] Robert Moeller and Mary Yates, *Africom's Deputies Visit*, http://ouagadougou.usembassy.gov/africomcom.html, 2008, 67-73, (accessed 15 Nov 2010).

[127] U.S. Africa Command J5, Discussion with SAMS Fellows. Lecture, Kelly Barracks,Germany. Nov 2010.

[128] Development that focused on the challenges of creating a new, regional command part-and-parcel from an existing command without the equal distribution of support and resources previously required in the region.

[129] U.S. Africa Command J5, Discussion with SAMS Fellows. Lecture, Kelly Barracks,Germany. Nov 2010.

Joint Staff. Since a large portion of US forces are committed to the cyclical requirements in Iraq and Afghanistan, it is largely believed that the only way to apportion military forces to USAFRICOM will be at direct intervention of, or reaction to, a terrorist act on the homeland or to a crisis intervention on the continent. Second, Africa is not a suitable theater for indirect military intervention. One must be invited by the host nation to intervene and, as determined by the political agendas of the 53 member states of the African Union (AU), this invitation is not forthcoming. Finally, the lack of capacity in this austere region means that everything, from logistics to operations, is inherently inefficient.[130]

The ultimate purpose of USAFRICOM is to support US foreign policy from the whole-of-government approach. As such, USAFRICOM appears to transcend military responsibilities with the task to use all the elements of national power. The USAFRICOM leadership attempts to accomplish this by employing the principle of Active Security to support humanitarian-assistance efforts, to provide crisis response, and to promote a stable and secure African environment.[131] Active Security requires a holistic approach through interagency cooperation and the ability to conduct operations with well-trained, disciplined armies who respect the rule of law. These initiatives should be through diplomacy and international organizations with trusted, reliable partners, not through military engagement and institution building.[132] Proactive peacetime engagement could lead to prosperity and stability, which is in line with the diplomatic and political missions in the African region. [133]

A Recommendation for Future Commands

The current draft UCP realigns boundaries to more clearly reflect geographic responsibilities. These adjustments are expected within geographic unified commands, but these adjustments also suggest functional unified commands could benefit from realigning to more clearly reflect functional

---

[130] Carter F. Ham, U.S. Africa Command's Written Statement Online to the House Armed Services Committee, 112th Congress, Apr 2011, 28-29, available at http://www.africom.mil/pdfFiles/PostureStatement.pdf, (accessed 26 Apr 2011).

[131] Ham, 10-11.

[132] Ham, 16-17.

[133] Ham, 31.

responsibilities. A more regional focus on national security and homeland defense and a rise of complex, global threats (weapons of mass destruction, terrorism, cyber-attack, etc.) may require senior leaders to rethink the number and type of unified commands that are required to contend with the US' global security challenges. The entering argument should always be bounded by the fact that operations are planned and conducted by joint forces under the direction of the commanders, not by the military Services, defense agencies, or Pentagon staffs.[134]

Re-visits to the UCP are fairly typical after major events take place. For example, after the fall of the Soviet Union and the so-called peace dividend, the administration directed a Roles and Missions Commission to make recommendations to improve joint operations, resource allocation, and structure of the UCP.[135] The following is typical language used when studying and making recommendations for changing the UCP:

America's future will be marked by rapid change, diverse contingencies, limited budgets and a broad range of missions to support evolving national security policies. Providing military capabilities that operate effectively together to meet future challenges is the common purpose of the military departments, the Services, the defense agencies and other DOD elements. All must focus on DOD's real product--effective military operations.[136]

To be successful, the commander must combine unified forces from an array of capabilities provided to them. This means that the commanders must have a role in helping determine the capabilities that will be available. This also requires the close cooperation within DOD, the Services, and the support agencies. The DOD has strengthened its capabilities for unified operations since passage of the Goldwater-Nichols Act.[137] But that mission is not yet complete. Restructuring commands based on function to ensure effective joint operations is essential to a successful and secure future. The goal is effective unified military operations.

---

[134] Directions for Defense: Report of the Commission on Roles and Missions of the Armed Forces, (Washington D.C.: Government Printing Office, 1994), iii

[135] Ibid.

[136] Directions for Defense, Roles and Missions Commission of the Armed Forces, Report to Congress, the SECDEF, and the Chairman of the Joint Chiefs of Staff, 24 May 1995, available at http://www. fas.org/man /docs/corm95/di1062.html (accessed 15 Mar 2011).

[137] Ibid.

A plethora of articles and essays are written recommending different courses of action to change the UCP. The recommendations vary in degree but the recurring theme of the literature is the number of recommendations appears to equal the number of articles written. The following proposed functional structure of the UCP is not new. An article published by Major Houlgate had similar ideas and constructs in 2005 called *A Unified Command Plan for a New Era.* The author used the argument behind this functional construct for this discussion.[138] The difference lies within the proposed structure of the JTF, the number of commands proposed, as well as not diminishing the role of each Service.

The Proposal

Today's world is undeniably interconnected. Having senior commanders focus on specific regions cheats reality. Terrorism, natural disasters, and other challenges (among them weapons of mass destruction and non-proliferation, space, information, and communications) have no borders. Removing geography from operational command also removes the stigma created by bounding regions together that otherwise might not be, or excluding regions that otherwise should be. This plan can place the regional focus and initiative back into the hands of the State Department, the NSC, and interagency process. To account for this, the proposal recommends creating four additional functional commands in conjunction with the current three, while eliminating all of the regional commands. The Joint Staff remains as a staffing function.

In this proposal, the Homeland Defense Command (USHDCOM) focuses on defending the US homeland, to include borders and coastlines. This command would work closely with the Department of Homeland Security, the Coast Guard, and nations north and south of our borders. The Humanitarian Assistance and Disaster Relief Command (USHADRCOM) would have close ties to non-governmental organizations, PVOs, and the civil disaster-relief communities. The Security and Stability (USSSCOM) would operate the US' security cooperation and engagement efforts worldwide, to include stability and

---

[138] Changing DOD is a continuing strategic challenge for the future. Years of war are stretching the Armed Forces thin (in people, equipment, training cycles, etc.). Numerous articles are published with recommendations to change the UCP. In short, it is difficult to find a new idea but not in implementing the construct on the whole.

reconstruction missions. The War Command (USWARCOM) would train to fight the nation's major, conventional high-intensity combat efforts.

The Joint Staff would remain for experimentation, exercises focused on future conflict, and working any changes required by law. The current functional commands (Special Forces, Strategic, and Transportation) would retain much of their current missions, with changes as needed to balance the new plan. In this construct, the joint trainer and force provider would be the Joint Staff with the inherent support from each of the Services.[139]

In this example, geographic commands are no longer included. The Services would still organize, train, and equip forces to provide to the functional commands. Each commander would be required to maintain a rapidly deployable JTF headquarters cell. In the event of a crisis, the SECDEF would assign a supported command and give instructions. A task force focused on a narrow set of operational tasks and missions means that each JTF would be better prepared to accomplish its assigned mission. As such, the combatant commander's primary means for responding to an emerging crisis are the capabilities-based JTF. Joint Publication 0-2 states that a JTF can be established by the SECDEF, a combatant commander, or an existing JTF commander.[140] This gives the commander authority to organize forces to best accomplish the assigned mission based on the concept of operations.[141] Joint Pub 3-0 enables combatant commanders to "directly control the conduct of military operations or delegate that authority to a subordinate commander."[142] When viewed through the lens of joint doctrine, command and control, and interoperability, the JTF with a permanent staff is the preferable choice. The JTF improves mission capabilities while reducing many of the inefficiencies associated with the regional commands.

---

[139] Kelly Houlgate, *A Unified Command Plan for a New Era*, The Naval Institute: Proceedings, Sep 2005, available at http://www.military.com NewContent/0,13190,NI_0905_Uni,00 html, (accessed 15 Nov 2010).

[140] Joint Publication 0-2, *Unified Action Armed Forces* (UNAAF), (Washington, D.C.: Government Printing Office, 2006) II-6.

[141] Ibid.

[142] Joint Publication 3-0, *Doctrine for Joint Operations*, (Washington, D.C.: Government Printing Office, 2008), III-.

For example, the Special Operations Command established and activated a standing JTF in 1989. This JTF executes the nation's dedicated counter-terrorist missions.[143] The experience gained in creating this JTF increased interagency and joint staff interoperability. The success of this Special Operations Command over the years displays how a unified command, with a dedicated JTF, can accomplish a specific function without regard to geographic boundaries. Using these lessons and applying them to the current proposal, each commander could focus on a capability or functional area. This would permit the DOD to mass efforts towards expertise and economy of force. For example, the USHADRCOM staff would be populated with members of the Services and various interagency partners whose training and expertise are dedicated towards humanitarian operations. The USSSCOM would be filled with language experts and warriors with small wars skill sets. The USSOCOM would continue to focus on direct-action missions against high-value targets, but many Special Forces capabilities might move to USSSCOM to minimize capability gaps. Because of the structure of each functional command within this proposal, the SECDEF could allocate missions in order to minimize risk. Links to each Service, based on traditional roles and missions, would likely shift as the plan matures.

Some readers may discount this proposal simply due to its jarring change to the normal comfort zone. For example, to understand the region and know the context firsthand, the command (and its people) must be located in the region. The counter argument is at least threefold: First, the global speed and process power of information awareness supports a functional command structure. Geography no longer constrains operational commanders. Additionally, only the Pacific (hindered by the 'tyranny of distance') and the European commands have their primary headquarters in their theater of responsibility. For example, Central Command leads its Middle East mission from a headquarters in Florida. Second, with a revitalized NSC, all the elements of national power could be better aligned. The Council can organize itself for specific tasks, by region if required. Therefore, the State and Defense Departments could also have regional teams to advise their leaders. This might form the core of the US Government's

---

[143] James R. Helmy, *Future U.S. Strategy: The Need for a Standing Joint Task Force*, Unpublished Research Paper, (Carlisle, PA: U.S. Army War College, 1991), 22.

geographic expertise, which could be augmented by a continuous flow of global intelligence. State Department country teams will remain crucial parts of the process by responding to requests for information on their specific nations, as well as joining in the solution process. Finally, combatant commanders currently focus efforts on continually tracking regional trends and planning for contingency missions.[144] Under this proposal, commanders would provide capabilities to accomplish assigned missions--perhaps focusing on specific regions, but mostly on mission sets--with significant participation from the NSC interagency community. The US Government as a whole would then focus regionally and globally, while DOD focuses on needed military response capabilities.[145]

Critics might point out that the commands under this fictitious plan appear to duplicate Service roles. This is a valid point. A common criticism of SOCOM, despite its success, is that it has almost become a fifth service. That perception is primarily because it trains and equips forces, traditionally Service roles, for specific missions. This is exactly what commanders under the proposed plan would do. Services would still have to provide forces across the spectrum of commands and would thus not be as specialized. As with SOCOM today, the commanders and Services could share training costs and maximize opportunities. The ultimate result might be the marginalization of each Service...truthfully the single issue that leads to heavy resistance to change. With this plan, however, there are not many compelling arguments to maintain Services as they currently exist in an era of joint warfare and soon-to-be joint procurement. Taking away some of the acquisition authorities (the "equip" of "organize, train, and equip") from the Services, and giving them to the new commanders, would potentially alleviate many of the programmatic dilemmas facing the DOD and Congress. Commanders, focused solely on their specific required capabilities, would not compete as aggressively. Of course there would still be budget

---

[144] Kelly Houlgate, A Unified Command Plan for a New Era, The Naval Institute: Proceedings, Sep 2005, available at http://www military.com NewContent/0,13190,NI_0905_Uni,00 html, (accessed 15 Nov 2010).

[145] Ibid.

battles, but once capability requirements were set by the SECDEF, it would primarily be a mathematics problem, not a roles-and-missions debate.[146]

This plan can place the regional focus and initiative back into the hands of the State Department, the NSC, and interagency process. To be sure, the interagency community might need to reorganize to include regional interagency teams, but the DOD command structure interface would be streamlined significantly. For example, a single command, Security and Stability, would work closely with the State Department to manage security cooperation efforts and global engagement. Challenging issues, such as the current division of the Caribbean and Africa and the Israel-Arab Middle East dilemma, now under two separate commands, could be re-evaluated by not being tied to geographic boundaries. Perhaps most importantly, DOD could focus on the world as a whole, not in packets. The likely nature of the *Age of Persistent Conflict* continuing over generations (not to mention other recent trends in North Africa and the Middle East) begs for boundary-free organizations.

Benefits to Functional Commands

The proposal of the UCP may not be the best answer to future security concerns that the US faces. One concern is this proposal struggles to match unity of effort to achieve interagency and joint coordination as discussed with the USAFRICOM example. As such, the DOD will need to take the lead to reform the interagency process. A great place to start would be reforming the UCP. However, the conceptual question to answer with any change to the plan is: does the UCP, as structured or as proposed, serve an effective purpose and provide an adequate command-and-control apparatus for contingency, security, and stability operations across the globe? The discussion of Africa is sufficiently limiting and important as one region normally neglected by the UCP. The current UCP provides a less-than-adequate structure to conduct military operations in support of US policy objectives to adhere to the National Security Strategy for the region. Because of this, the utility and effectiveness of the current UCP as a split between regional and functional focus remains in question.

---

[146] Ibid.

On the other hand, the discussion of SOCOM is truly the test case for the proposed realignment. It is a functional command that has an operational and strategic war-fighting mission and it has a much larger budget than the other commands. It seems to be passing this test with muster. This is largely due to SOCOM's uniqueness within the UCP and its budget. To be blunt, making many from the one will disenfranchise the capabilities that were produced from making the one from many. In this case, there can be too much of a good thing.

However, the future appears to call for command structures that will better prepare the nation's armed forces to conduct the most likely missions across the globe. As it has done many times in the past, the DOD should take this opportunity to exercise some rigorous thought on the possibilities of unified command.

Revisions and Changes

Changing the UCP is not a radical idea but it is a parochial one. Partly because the history of the UCP involves debates over how the component commands should be organized. These disputes usually pitted those who wanted commands organized by geographic areas against those who advocated forming commands according to functional groupings of forces.[147] Change is a normal, periodic process by which the Defense Department re-evaluates military strategy to support national security interests. The UCP is a flexible document designed to adapt to changing times. The most recent changes created Northern Command and eliminated Joint Forces Command. It appears as though the DOD is currently at a crossroads of opportunity for significant change. For example, in the last six months alone, the DOD published the Quadrennial Defense Review; the administration has called for global realignment of forces; the President is in the midst of reorganizing the war on terror; government officials and outside observers call for increased interagency cooperation throughout government; Congress is focused on balanced budgets and debt elimination; and the *Age of Persistent Conflict* appears to be a struggle that

---

[147] Inferred over the last 2 decades of UCP changes with the resultant 6/4 split of regional to functional combatant commands.

will last well beyond the current plan. The convergence of these factors means the US must increase security, increase efficiency, and better train and prepare to respond to future crisis. This will require significant changes to the UCP.

Conclusion

For over sixty years, unified command incrementally changed in what appears to be an attempt to maximize US military power and influence both regionally and globally. Perhaps the best way to maximize this effectiveness is for the entire "security establishment" to follow suit. The combining of all the national instruments of power within the US system of civilian control over the military will potentially revitalize the entire National Security Strategy (and structure) to fully integrate policy with power. This could create a global system to advance freedom, peace, and prosperity fostered by the UCP structure.[148] In review, to be more efficient and effective, it is not only appropriate for the UCP to shift from a regional focus to a functional focus, but it would be more appropriate for the entire national security structure to align each of the elements of national power within similar structures, thereby fostering cooperation and engagement.

Reliance on all the available instruments of national power is vital to the US National Security Strategy. In studying the history of, and maturation of, unified command in the military displays how cultural, philosophical, doctrinal, and organizational differences among Services (as well as among other government agencies) present problems to efficiency and effectiveness. The traditional military structure used to enforce foreign policy is no longer suitable for all the challenges of the future. There is no longer a single military solution. The DOD will require coordination and cooperation internal to the Services as well as external with interagency partners. The mantra of whole-of-government approach will mean either the NSC coordinates government activities through an established interagency process/structure by providing a strategic mechanism for policy development, or the government relies on coordination of interagency efforts at the operational and tactical levels.

---

[148] Cronin, 1.

The DOD wrestled with unity of effort and joint military operations since the Spanish-American War. Throughout this history, the military in general realized that unity of effort and unity of command are vitally important when aligned to efficient and effective joint military operations. The lessons learned over the history of unified command can provide valuable suggestions for unifying the National Security Strategy among the responsible government and non-government agencies. The coordination relies on understanding the intricacies of both the regional and functional capabilities of each combatant command and how they might align with the different government agencies. The new international security environment is dynamic and uncertain, with recurring disputes, crises, and conflicts in many regions as well as pervasive conflicts in regions of particular importance to the US[149] United States military overseas presence will remain, providing security cooperation and assistance will remain, training and exercises with allies and partner nations will remain…in short, the current UCP is structured to ensure the US military strategy maintains globally secure while promoting regional stability in line with the current National Security Strategy. But the current UCP is not structured to ensure efficient operations across the entire national security establishment.

Anticipating Service opposition, what is the value of proposing changes to the UCP? First, theater commanders charged with executing military and humanitarian missions supporting national policy vital to the US are more flexible and responsive, and have more forces than before. Second, boundaries and seams are de-conflicted between commands and crosstalk among commands is increased. Third, requirements of fixed, military alliances are differentiated from bilateral and multilateral agreements. Finally, it preserves strategic flexibility through the concentration of the rapid deployment and reserve forces.[150]

---

[149] Joint Publication 1, *Doctrine for the Armed Forces of the United States*, (Washington D.C.: Government Printing Office, May 2007), vii.

[150] John T. Quinn, *Toward a New Strategic Framework: A Unified Command Plan for the New World Order*, Defense Technical Information Center, Naval Postgraduate School, Monterey, California; Dec 1993, 163-164.

Research for this monograph has shown there is no shortage of literature and ideas on changing the UCP. Research for this monograph has also shown a service-parochial propensity for reigniting arguments over old disputes when re-examining the UCP from an organizational perspective. The most successful approach, based on historical changes to the UCP, is the current philosophy of implementing incremental and sustainable change so the geographic combatant commanders can accomplish functional missions and the functional combatant commanders can accomplish missions globally. Preserving Service identity at the division, wing, and battle-group levels is paramount to any recommended changes to the UCP. Regardless, unity of command must remain structured, both within the DOD and within the military Services, to accomplish the objectives outlined in the National Security Strategy and National Military Strategy. The UCP is the vehicle to reform the military in increments and precipitate change throughout the Department of Defense.

Appendix A

Major Legislative Changes to the UCP

Congressional oversight with regard to the joint operations of the Services, especially during constrained budgets, is always in the forefront of any discussion when programming monies. Consideration for the "out years" for research, development, acquisition, and procurement plays a major role in these discussions. The UCP is one method for the US Congress to act directly with the DOD. To be clear, the UCP is an executive document signed by the President of the US As of late, changes to the UCP recommended by the CJCS are reviewed by the SECDEF.[151] These changes typically address military concerns with regard to the global environment; threat lay-down, force structure, and joint-military organization. The UCP also serves as a measure of the Services' capabilities (and desire) to become more joint.[152]

Normally, Congressional concerns are addressed and incorporated with the CJCS recommendations to change to the UCP. However, throughout the DOD's history, if Congressional concerns were not addressed adequately, then the Congress voted to take legislative action. These modifications to the UCP addressed the interests and concerns of Congress both domestically and abroad. Congressional concerns are normally strategic. Recent examples of influence include weapons of mass destruction and nonproliferation, terrorism, space, national missile defense, and cyberspace. From this list, it is clear that threats and pressure have the potential to change military organizations. As a background to understand the current UCP, the following benchmark Congressional and military initiatives which drastically changed the UCP since its inception are presented for review.[153]

---

[151] Approved by the President, the UCP sets forth basic guidance to unified commanders; establishes missions, functions, and force structure; and delineates geographic areas of responsibility (AOR). Under section 161 of Title 10 of the U.S. Code, as added by the Goldwater-Nichols Department of Defense Reorganization Act of 1986, the CJCS must review the UCP not less than every 2 years for missions, responsibilities, and force structure. The CJCS must recommend changes through the SECDEF to the President.

[152] William C. Story, *Military Changes to the Unified Command Plan: Background and Issues for Congress*, (Congressional Research Service: The Library of Congress, June 1999), 1-2.

[153] Prior to Congressional reports, a UCP working group from the Joint Staff, unified commands, and service representatives debate UCP issues and developed a list of pros and cons for each issue. Issues are then

The National Security Act of 1947

After the success of WWII, President Truman approved the Outline Command Plan. This plan, considered by many as the first UCP, established seven unified commands with guiding principles relating to authorities and structure. This Plan created the legal foundation for dividing the globe into military areas of responsibility with each command responsible to the SECDEF and the President.[154] Under the original plan, each of the unified commands operated with one of the Service Chiefs (the Chief of Staff of the Army or Air Force, or Chief of Naval Operations) serving as an executive agent representing the JCS.[155]

The Key West Agreements of 1948

The Key West Agreement is the informal name for a new policy of the Armed Forces and the JCS. Its most prominent feature was an outline for the division of air assets between the Army, Navy, and the newly created Air Force that, with modifications, continues to provide the basis for the division of these assets in the US military today.

The Department of Defense Reorganization Act of 1958

After the Korean War, and understanding the operational lessons learned from the Middle East though 1957, President Eisenhower concluded that, from here on out, combat actions would be joint. Therefore, this Act unified all military planning, military command, and combat forces. The President, through the SECDEF, could establish unified and specified commands, assign missions, and lay down force structure. The chain of command ran from the President through the SECDEF and to combatant

---

analyzed and, if considered to be particularly contentious, are recommended for congressional review (this assumes the CJCS cannot satisfactorily mediate the contention). The Joint Staff refines all the UCP issues and related pros and cons to developed specific options and recommendations changes to the UCP for the CJCS review. Typically, collective military judgment is sent forth in the UCP for presidential signature.

[154] Ronald H. Cole, et. al., *The History of the Unified command Plan, 1946-1993*, (Washington D.C.: Joint History Office, Office of the Chairman of the Joint Chiefs of Staff, 1995), 12-15.

[155] Joint Chiefs of Staff *"History of the Unified Command Plan, 1977-1983,"* (July 1985), http://www.dod.gov/pubs/foi/reading_room/269.pdf. accessed 21 August 2010.

commanders. These commanders were given full operational control over assigned forces that remained in place. The JCS served under the SECDEF in a staff function.[156]

1974-1975 Review

This is one of the first major internal reviews to re-appraise and restructure the unified and specified commands in light of current political attitudes, manpower, and budget realities due to the end of the Vietnam War and impending energy crisis. In addition, strategic concepts for security and US interests were introduced in light of Cold War tensions.[157]

Steadman Report of 1977

This report recommended establishing a mandatory biennial review of the UCP every two years to respond more efficiently and effectively to the increasing rapid evolution of political and military realities. It was adopted in 1979. Additionally, Rapid Deployment Force (today's JTF) was created to respond in the Persian Gulf region in light of lessons learned from the Arab-Israeli War of 1973, political and social unrest in Iran, Pakistan, and Afghanistan (power vacuum), and OPEC controlling oil prices.[158] This force later became CENTCOM.

Department of Defense Authorization Act of 1982

In a different light, and at the request of the Army and Navy, Congress codified into law prohibiting the use of funds for integrating the Army's Military Traffic Management Command and the Navy's Military Sealift Command into a new transportation command, which the JCS desired. Later repealed, the bill effectively prohibited joint and unified transportation operations over land and sea.[159]

---

[156] Cole, 28.

[157] Cole, 43.

[158] Cole, 66.

[159] Cole, 101.

(Goldwater-Nichols) Department of Defense Reorganization Act of 1986

This Act directed the CJCS to review missions, responsibilities, force structure, and geographic

boundaries of each combatant command every two years by law and to recommend changes to the

President through the SECDEF. The powers of the CJCS and unified and specified commands were

expanded along with greater interaction with Congress and the budget process.[160]

Commission on Roles and Missions of the Armed Forces

In 1994, Congress established this commission to review the efficacy and appropriateness for the

post-Cold War era of the current allocations of roles, missions, and functions; evaluate and report on

alternative allocations of those roles, missions, and functions; and make recommendations for changes in

the current definition and distribution of each.[161] Traditional service methods for this allocation lead to

institutional quarrels and lack of compromise. Congress intended to improve joint operations with this

Act.[162]

Numerous other biennial changes to the UCP took place over the course of sixty years but the

previous actions show how Congress altered the way the military and DOD handle the UCP. The creation

of SOCOM; the creation and subsequent elimination of Joint Forces Command, Space Command, and

Atlantic Command; and the recent creation of USAFRICOM are all examples of other changes to the

UCP brought about by global change.

For the immediate future, the split requirements and numbers of the regional and functional

combatant commanders is about right. In other words, the military doesn't expect a radical change to the

UCP in the near term. The senior military leaders expect incremental changes to the UCP as an

evolutionary approach that aligns the UCP with the National Security Strategy and the National Military

---

[160] Cole, 96-102.

[161] P.L. 103-160, H.R. 2401, *National Defense Authorization Act for FY 1994*, Sec 953 (a), 107 STAT. 1738.

[162] Directions for Defense: Report of the Commission on Roles and Missions of the Armed Forces, (Washington, D.C.: government Printing Office, 1994), iii.

Strategy. These documents are the current vision of a notional future that the UCP attempts to take into account.

BIBLIOGRAPHY

Books

Allard, Kenneth C., *Command, Control, and the Common Defense*, New Haven, CT: Yale University Press, 1990.

Barnett, Thomas P.M., *The Pentagon's New Map, War and Peace in the Twenty-First Century*, New York, NY: GP Putman's Sons, 2004.

Bouchard, Joseph F. *Command in Crisis : Four Case Studies.* New York: Columbia University Press, 1991.

Brecher, Michael, and Jonathan Wilkenfeld. *A Study of Crisis.* Ann Arbor: University of Michigan Press, 1997.

Cohen, Elliot A., *Gulf War Air Power Survey,* Washington, D.C.: Joint History Office, 1993, Vol II, Part II.

Drew, Dennis, *Making Strategy: An Introduction to National Security Processes and Problems*, Honolulu, Hawaii: University Press of the Pacific, 2002.

Friedman, Thomas L., *The World is Flat, A Brief History of the Twenty-First Century*, New York: Farrar, Straus & Giroux, 2005.

Gordon, Michael R., and Bernard E. Trainor. *The Generals' War: The Inside Story of the Conflict in the Gulf.* 1st ed. Boston: Little, Brown, 4802.

Halberstam, David. War in a Time of Peace: Bush, Clinton, and the Generals. New York: Scribner, 2001.

Herspring, Dale R. The Pentagon and the Presidency: Civil-Military Relations from FDR to George W. Bush. Lawrence: University Press of Kansas, 2005.

Huntington, Samuel P., "Organization and Strategy," *Public Interest*, Spring 1984. Reprinted in *Reorganizing America's Defenses: Leadership I War and Peace* (Robert J. Art, Vincent Davis, and Samuel P. Huntington, Editors), Washington D.C.: Pergamon-Brassey's, 1985.

Matloff, Maurice and Edwin M. Snell, *The United States Army in World War II: The War Department: Strategic Planning for Coalition Warfare, 1941-1942*, Washington, DC: Office of the Chief of Military History, Department of the Army, 1953.

Murdock, Clark A., and Maichele A. Flournoy. *Beyond Goldwater-Nichols: U.S. Government and Defense Reform for a New Strategic Era.* Phase 2 Report. Washington, DC: Center For Strategic and International Studies, July 2005.

Penn, Dennis R., *Africa Command and the Militarization of U.S. Foreign Policy*, Washington D.C.: Department of Defense, July 2003.

Priest, Dana. The Mission: Waging War and Keeping Peace with America's Military. 1st ed. New York: WW Norton, 2003.

Poole, Kenneth H., *USSOCOM Research Topics 2011*, Joint Special Operations University, Hurlburt Field, FL: Government Printing Office, June 2010.

Schnabel, James F., *The History of the Joint Chiefs of Staff: The Joint Chiefs of Staff and National Policy: Volume I: 1945-1947*, Washington, D.C.: Historical Division, Joint Secretariat, Joint Chiefs of Staff, 1979.

Periodicals

Boyer, Peter J. "The New War Machine: A Reporter at Large." *The New Yorker* 79, no. 17 (Jun 30 2003): 055.

Canby, Steven L. "Roles, Missions, and JTFs: Unintended Consequences." *Joint Force Quarterly*, (Autumn/Winter 1994-95): 68-75

Clark, Wesley K. Waging Modern War: Bosnia, Kosovo, and the Future of Combat. 1st ed. New York: Public Affairs, 2001.

Cohen, William S. *Kosovo: Operation Allied Force: After-Action Report.* Washington: Department of Defense, 2000.

Cropsey, Seth. "The Limits of Jointness." *Joint Force Quarterly* (Summer 1993): 72-79.

Fatua, David T. "The Paradox of Joint Culture." *Joint Force Quarterly* (Autumn 2000): 81-86.

Fergueson, David W., and Bobby E. Glisson. "Opportunities for Military Services to Consolidate Support Functions." *Air Force Journal of Logistics* (Fall 1993): 19-24.

Flores, Susan L. "JTF's: Some Practical Implications." *Joint Force Quarterly* (Spring 1995): 111-113.

Gregor, William J., *Toward a Revolution in Civil-Military Affairs: Understanding the United States Military in the Post-Cold War World*, Working paper No. 6, Harvard University: John M. Olin Institute for Strategic Studies, Aug 1996, 19.

Hines, Scott M. "Standing Down a Joint Task Force." *Joint Force Quarterly* (Autumn/Winter 1994/1995): 111-116.

Hooker, Richard D. Jr. "America's Two Armies." *Joint Force Quarterly* (Autumn/Winter 1994/95): 38-46.

Huntington, Samuel P., "Organization and Strategy," *Public Interest*, Spring 1984. Reprinted in *Reorganizing America's Defenses: Leadership I War and Peace* (Robert J. Art, Vincent Davis, and Samuel P. Huntington, Editors), Washington D.C.: Pergamon-Brassey's, 1985, 250-251.

Lovelace, Douglas C. Jr., "The DOD Reorganization Act of 1986: Improving the Department through Centralization and Integration." In *Organizing for National Security*, ed. Douglas T. Stuart, Strategic Studies Institute, Nov 2000, 84.

Mackubin, Thomas Owens. "Accountable vs. Strategists: The New Roles and Missions Debate." *Strategic Review* (Fall 1992): 7-10.

Mulholland, John F. Jr., "Countering Irregular Threats: The Army Special Operations Contribution." *Joint Forces Quarterly*, 1st quarter 2010, 71.

Nunn, Sam. "DOD Reorganization: An Historical Perspective." *Armed Forces Journal International* 123, no.4, (October 1985): 15.

Pruher, Joseph W., "Rethinking the Joint Doctrine Hierarchy," *Joint Forces Quarterly*. Winter 1996-97, 43.

Staudenmaier, William O., "Contemporary Problems of the Unified Command System," *Parameters* Carlisle, PA: US Army War College, 1979, 93.

Government Documents

Cole, Ronald H. *The History of the Unified Command Plan, 1946-1999.* Washington, D.C.: Joint History Office, Office of the Chairman of the Joint Chiefs of Staff, 2003.

Cole, Ronald H. *The History of the Unified Command Plan, 1946-1993.* Washington, DC: Joint History Office, Office of the Chairman of the Joint Chiefs of Staff, 1996.

Department of Defense Directive Number 5100.01, *Functions of the Department of Defense and its Major Components*, Washington D.C.: Government Printing Office, Dec 2010, 21-25.

Gates, Robert M., Dr., *Strategic Communications and Information Operations in the DoD*, 25 Jan 2011, Memorandum For Record, The SECDEF, Washington D.C.

Joint Pub 3-0, *Doctrine for Joint Operations*, Washington, D.C.: Government Printing Office, 2008.

National Security Council, *Handbook for Interagency Management of Complex Contingency Operations*, Washington, DC: Government Printing Office, August 2008.

National Security Strategy 2010, Washington D.C.: The White House, May 2010.

National Security Council 68. *United States Objectives and Programs for National Security*. The White House. Washington, D.C. April 14, 1950. Available at http://www.fas.org/irp/offdocs/nsc-hst/nsc-68.htm.

National Security Decision Directive 32. *US National Security Strategy*. The White House. Washington, D.C. May 20, 1982. Available at http://www.fas.org/irp/offdocs/nsdd/nsdd-032.htm.

National Security Presidential Directive 1. *Organization of the National Security Council System*. The White House. Washington, D.C. February 13, 2001. Available at http://www.fas.org/irp/offdocs/nspd/index.html.

Presidential Decision Directive 56. *Managing Complex Contigency Operations*. The White House. Washington, D.C. May 1997. Available at http://www.fas.org/irp/offdocs/pdd/index.html.

President's Blue Ribbon Commission on Defense Management. *A Quest for Excellence: Final Report to the President*. Washington D.C., June 1986.

Public Papers of the Presidents of the United States, *Statement on the National Security Council Structure*, Washington D.C.: Government Printing Office, 1982.

Staff Report to the Committee on Armed Services, United States Senate, Defense Organization: The Need for Change, Washington DC: Government Printing Office, 1991, 277-279.

Story, William C, *Military Changes to the Unified Command Plan: Background and Issues for Congress*, Congressional Research Service: The Library of Congress, June 1999.

Unified Command Plan (DRAFT 2010), Washington D.C.: The White House, Government Printing Office, 2010.

U.S. Congress, Goldwater-Nichols Department of Defense Reorganization Act of 1986, Pub L. 99-433.

U.S. Congress. Goldwater-Nichols Department of Defense Reorganization Act of 1986. Public Law 99-433. Washington, DC: GPO, 1986.

U.S. Congress. House of Representatives. Goldwater-Nichols Department of Defense Reorganization Act of 1986 Conference Report (To Accompany H. R. 3622). Washington, DC: GPO, 1986.

U.S. Congress. Senate. Armed Services Committee. *General Norton A. Schwartz, USAF Confirmation Hearing.* 109th Cong., 1st sess., July 28, 2005.

United States. Congress. *Goldwater-Nichols Department of Defense Reorganization Act of 1986 Conference Report* (To Accompany H. R. 3622). Washington, DC: GPO, 1986. Y1.1/8:99-824. House Conference Report no. 99-824.

U.S. Congress. House. Armed Services Committee. *Hearings on National Defense Authorization Act for FY2002.* 106th Cong., 2nd Session, 28 March 2001.

_____. Senate. Committee on Appropriations. *Department of Defense Appropriations, FY91.* 101st Cong., 6 March 1990.

U.S. President. *National Security Strategy of the United States.* The White House. Washington D.C. Barrack Obama, June 2010. Available at http://www.fas.org/man/docs/918015-nss.htm.

_____. *The National Security Strategy of the United States.* The White House. Washington D.C. George W. Bush, September 2002.

_____. *The National Security Strategy of the United States.* The White House. Washington D.C. George W. Bush, March 2006.

——. JP 1, Doctrine for the Armed Forces of the United States. Washington, DC: GPO, 2007.

——. *JP 3-0, Joint Operations.* Washington, DC: GPO, 2006.

——. JP 5-0, Joint Operation Planning. Washington, DC: GPO, 2006.

U.S. Congress. Senate. *Public Law 99-433, Department of Defense Reorganization Act of 1986.* 99th Congress., 2d Sess., Washington, D.C.: Government Printing Office,1986.

_____. *Support of the Headquarters of Combatant and Subordinate Joint Commands.* Directive 5100.3. Washington, D.C.: Government Printing Office, March 24, 2004. 48 (accessed January 24, 2010). 49

Other Sources

Bennett, John T. "Beyond Goldwater-Nichols' Group to Study Interagency Task Forces." *Inside the Pentagon* (September 23, 2004). http://www.chinfo.navy.mil/navpalib/.www/rhumblines/rhumblines219.doc (accessed ...).

Bellamy, Mark, *Africa Command: An Idea Whose Time has come?* (Internet accessed Feb 15, 2011).

Binnendijk, Hans, ed. *Transforming America's Military*. Publication of the Center for Technology and National Security Policy National Defense University. Washington, DC: National Defense University Press, 2002.

Bryden, Alan, *Challenges of Security Sector Governance in West Africa*, Geneva Center for the Democratic Control of Armed Forces, PDF available at pcaf.ch (accessed 15 Oct 2010).

Chairman of the Joint Chiefs of Staff, *History of the Joint Staff*. http://www.jcs.mil/ (accessed 15 Jan 11).

Crowe, Kenneth M. *Goldwater-Nichols Act: Time for Reform*. Carlisle Barracks, PA: U.S. Army War College, 2000.

Defense Base Closure and Realignment Commission: Final Report to the President. Washington, DC: GPO, 2005. http://www.brac.gov/finalreport.html (accessed September 9, 2010).

Directions for Defense: Report of the Commission on Roles and Missions of the Armed Forces, Washington D.C.: Government Printing Office, 1994.

Directions for Defense, Roles and Missions Commission of the Armed Forces, Report to Congress, the SECDEF, and the Chairman of the Joint Chiefs of Staff, 24 May 1995, available at http://www.fas.org/man /docs/corm95/di1062.html (accessed 15 Mar 2011).

Glenn, Russell W., "No More Principles of War?" *Parameters*, Spring 1998, 48-66. Available at http://www.au.af.mil/au/awc/awcgate/army/no_more_principles.htm (accessed 1 April 2011).

Ham, Carter F., U.S. Africa Command's Written Statement Online to the House Armed Services Committee, 112th Congress, Apr 2011, 28-29, available at http://www.africom.mil/pdfFiles/PostureStatement.pdf, (accessed 1 May 2011).

Helmly, James R. Future U.S. Military Strategy: The Need For a Standing Joint Task Force. Carlisle, PA: US Army War College, 1991. http://handle.dtic.mil/100.2/ADA237692 (accessed 15 Nov 2010).

Hayes, James E. III. Honing the Dagger: The Formation of a Standing Joint Special Operations Task Force Headquarters. School of Advanced Military Studies Monographs. Fort Leavenworth, KS: US Army Command and General Staff College, 2005. In CARL digital library, http://cgsc.cdmhost.com/cdm4/item_viewer.php?CISOROOT=/p4013coll3&CISOPTR=334&CISOBOX=1&REC=1 (accessed...).

Henchen, Michael L. Establishment of a Permanent Joint Task Force Head-Quarters: An Analysis of Sourcing a Command and Control Structure Capable of Executing Forced Entry Contingency Operations. Fort Leavenworth, Kansas: U.S. Army Command and General Staff College, 1993.

Hildenbrand, Marc R. Standing Joint Task Forces : A Way to Enhance America's Warfighting Capabilities?. School of Advanced Military Studies Monographs. Fort Leavenworth, KS: US Army Command and General Staff College, 1992. In CARL digital library, http://cgsc.cdmhost.com/cdm4/item_viewer.php?CISOROOT=/p4013coll3&CISOPTR=1559&CISOBOX=1&REC=6 (accessed…).

Houlgate, Kelly, *"A Unified Command Plan for a New Era," Proceedings*, The Naval Institute, Monterey, California; Sep 2005, available at http://www.military.com NewContent/ 0,13190, NI_0905_Uni,00.html, (accessed 15 Nov 2010).

Johnson, W. Spenser, *New Challenges for the Unified Command Plan*, Joint Forces Quarterly, Summer 2002, available at http://www.dtic.mil/doctrine/jel/jfq_pubs/1231.pdf, (accessed 15 Nov 2010).

Kohn, Richard H. "The Erosion of Civilian Control of the Military in the United States Today." *Naval War College Review* 55, no. 3 (2002).

Lawlor, Bruce M., *Military Support of Civil Authorities-A New Focus for a New Millennium*, October 2000 (Updated September 2001), available at http://www.homelandsecurity.org/journal/Articles/Lawlor.htm (accessed 26 Apr 2011).

Lovelace, Douglas C. Unification of the United States Armed Forces: Implementing the 1986 Department of Defense Reorganization Act. Carlisle Barracks, Pa.: Strategic Studies Institute, U.S. Army War College, 1996.

Morrison, Stephen J. and Kathleen Hicks, *Integrating 21st Century Development and Security Assistance, Final Report*; Center for Strategic and International Studies, Dec 2007.

Ploch, Lauren, *Africa Command US Strategic Interests and the Role of the US Military in Africa*; Library of Congress, July 6, 2007,updated Dec 7, 2007, (Internet accessed Nov 2010).

Quinn, John T., *Toward a New Strategic Framework: A Unified Command Plan for the New World Order*, Defense Technical Information Center, Naval Postgraduate School, Monterey, California; Dec 1993, 63-64.

The National Security Act of 1947, Available online at: http://www.state.gov/r/pa/ho/time/cwr/ 17603.htm, (accessed 15 Feb 2011).

U.S. Code Title 10, Armed Forces, Section 164. Available at http://uscode.house.gov /download /title_10.shtml (accessed 15 Nov 2010).

U.S. Department of Defense, Cyber Command Fact Sheet, May 21, 2010, http://www.stratcom. mil /factsheets/ cyber_Command,. (accessed 12 Feb 2011).

U.S. Department of Defense, Africa Command Fact Sheet, June 26, 2010, http://www.africom.mil/, accessed Oct 15, 2010.

USSOCOM Posture Statement. USSOCOM. 2007. Archived from the original on February 27, 2008. http://www.socom.mil/Docs/USSOCOM_Posture_Statement_2007.pdf. (Accessed 26 Apr 2011).

Wolf, Richard I. *The United States Air Force: Basic Documents on Roles and Missions.* Air Staff Historical Study, Office of Air Force History, Washington D.C., 1987.